WORDROBE MEDIA | FORWORD WRITER SERIES

PURGASTORY

5 Strategies For Escaping the Hell of Writer's Block

JONATHAN JORDAN

Wordrobe Media

This book is a work of nonfiction.

"If I waited for perfection, I would never write a word."

-Margaret Atwood

Need Some Writing Encouragement?
Subscribe here to receive some.

wordrobemedia.com/newsletter

TABLE OF CONTENTS

why this book exists.

You already know why this book exists. You probably don't need me to actually explain why. If you're a literate human (or dog or dolphin), then you've encountered that dreaded nemesis to all forms of word creation: writer's block.

But before we talk about writing, let's talk about science. Did you know there's no such thing as cold? We experience "cold" merely as the absence of heat energy. Heat is a thing—it's real. Cold? It's not a real thing. Rather, it's the *absence* of something that is real. The same thing with darkness. It's not a thing—it's the absence of light.

I believe the same concept is true for writer's block. It's not a thing. It's the absence of something. Accepting this fact is the first step to freedom from writer's block and also recognizing that it holds no power over us that we do not willingly give to it.

Okay, now we've talked about science, let's talk about faith—after all, it's not just for the sake of silly wordplay this book is titled *PurgaStory*. Now, I'm not Catholic, but to be fair to those who are, I will hereby recognize there is a common misconception about the idea of Purgatory. But I think this misconception has a lot to teach us about the nature of writer's block.

Pope Francis, if you're reading this, I'm open to correction if need be—but from my understanding, the idea of Purgatory is not actually a part of Hell as is often depicted, nor is it Hell Lite. Rather, it is an in-between place of purification for souls destined for glory. It's like a furnace that precious metal has to pass through to become more pure—not exactly the most pleasant place, but not the worst either. And I think that's what writer's block is like, to be honest.

We writers tend to make writer's block this big, scary hellish void from which there is no escape, when really, it can actually be good for a writer. It can actually be part of the creative process for us to find the good writing we are capable of doing. It's like waiting at the gate for your flight. Sure, you don't want to stay there forever, and it's not very pleasant when you are, but it's temporary and necessary to get you to your destination. Too often, we turn the idea of writer's block into something much scarier than what it is, and by doing so, we actually empower it instead of empowering ourselves to endure it.

Therefore, on the rare occasions writer's block enters my thoughts, I prefer to think of it as nothing more than an excuse preventing me from the writing process. Part of this is personal to me: I hate excuses. I'm a big believer that the best way to overcome a problem is to take ownership of the situation, not pass the buck or play the blame game. I'm also a big believer that nachos are the pinnacle of human food, so I'm rather wise, you see.

So here's the good news for you: by simply reading this book, you are taking ownership of the situation. You have taken the first step in re-orienting your mind concerning your writing and the excuses which keep you from doing what you say you love to do.

But simply reading this is not going to help you if you don't practice what I'm going to preach. That's what this book is really: a "sermon" to give you practical strategies on how to escape the hell of writer's block. To guide you along the treacherous path that leads out of PurgaStory. Amen.

Whether you believe in Purgatory or not, you probably wouldn't be here right now if you didn't believe in PurgaStory, aka "writer's block." But understanding its proper context is the first step in overcoming it. It is only as powerful as you make it and my hope in this book is to give you some strategies to take power back. When you're cold, you turn on the heat. When it's dark, you flip the light switch. The best way to fight writer's block is—you guessed it—to write.

But why me? What credentials do I have compared to any other self-proclaimed writing expert out there?

First off, I'm *not* an expert. And I've never self-proclaimed to be. But rather, I'll be the first to admit that craft of writing is never something you can finish learning. I'm still learning myself, but I enjoy sharing what I've learned. As of the writing of this updated edition, I'm a full-time book coach and ghostwriter. Beyond using these strategies for myself, I've taught them to other writers and have seen them benefit as a result.

In fact, I'd be remiss to not mention that this book owes a huge debt of gratitude to the article "8 Quotes To

Combat Writer's Block" published online by The Writer's Circle. While the article itself is never actually quoted, many of the great quotes in the article proved helpful, so they were incorporated into the text as necessary.

Second, I myself have struggled with writer's block. For example, it took me five minutes to finish this sentence. Could you tell? But the fact is I struggle with it far less now after implementing the strategies I'll share here.

There was a time not so long ago when my laptop was filled with twenty half-started, unfinished stories and notes I could not bring to fruition. But now, with these strategies, I have found ways to stay focused, find inspiration, and finish what I start. It would not be right to keep this to myself, not when it has proven so effective for me.

Third, my writing experience has spanned everything from blogging, freelance commercial work, copyediting, poetry, creative consulting, ghostwriting, playwriting and screenwriting. And at one point, I helped write the lyrics for an experimental opera. But you can't do that broad a range of writing and not develop ways to overcome writer's block. It becomes a necessity when you are working with deadlines and collaborating with others.

Fourth, because…no. There's no fourth. You should always (ALWAYS) only give three reasons for something. More than that is just too much, excessive, and extraneous. Not to mention redundant.

So my hope is that through this bite-sized book on writing, you'll do just that—more writing and less sitting around wishing you were writing. Best case scenario: you implement these strategies, write a masterpiece, and become rich and famous. Worst case scenario: you end up writing a book about how to deal with writer's block.

STRATEGY #1: the wisdom of clichés

"There is no greater agony than bearing an untold story inside you."

-Maya Angelou

The above quote is, in my opinion, anything but a cliché lest someone make the accusation. Rather, the great Maya Angelou's words are a great starting point for this strategy because this quote taps into the pain of the creative process—the yearning to get a feeling, an idea, a mission out of your brain and onto paper. That being said, there are some common writing clichés which offer possible solutions to escaping this agony and converting an *untold* story into a *told* story.

After all, clichés become clichés for a reason—often because there is at least some truth to them, because they have worked for someone somewhere. "If it ain't broke, don't fix it." There's a cliché quote for you. But it's true.

You could say the same about formulas. Writers worry all the time about their writing being too "formulaic," but the whole reason those formulas exist is because they work. They are proven. They get results. So there is a time and season for following a formula and you shouldn't have to feel guilty about that.

And that's why we're starting here. The clichés and formulas of writing are easy to remember and all too easy to ignore. But you shouldn't! There is a lot of wisdom to be found in them.

CLICHÉ #1: WRITE EVERY DAY

You should! You should write. Every. Day. Monday. Tuesday. Wednesday. Thursday. Birthday. Midday. Christmas Day. Even if you have to force yourself. And some days, you *will* have to force yourself.

Too often, writers think they need a lengthy chunk of uninterrupted time to write. Rubbish! Folderol! All you need is a writing utensil. The end.

Don't get me wrong. If you can get a lengthy chunk of uninterrupted time, then take it. But for many of us, that can be really difficult to come by, even impossible. So sometimes you may be writing during ten minutes of your lunch break, or the five minutes you have in-between appointments. Or on your phone in the bathroom stall, and then emailing yourself the notes for later on. Sometimes that's what writing takes, whether you do it full-time, part-time, or some-time.

You might be wondering how this helps with writer's block. Turns out, the mere act of writing—especially disciplined writing—helps you evade writer's block.

So do whatever you have to do to obey the cliché: set an alarm on your phone, lock yourself in a closet as your toddler screams for sustenance. Okay, ignore that last one. Don't do anything that will put anyone in harm's way or get you arrested. But you get the point.

There's one exception to this rule—and I hesitate to mention it—but here it is: if you're not writing, you should be *researching*, because it's hard to write if you don't research. Which leads us to our next cliché…

CLICHÉ #2: WRITE WHAT YOU KNOW

I freely admit I used to scoff at this particular cliché. In fact, I downright struggled and fought with myself over including it here. My brain said, "There's nothing more boring to write about than 'what you know.'" For the longest time, I thought this cliché meant writers could only write about their own experiences, that my characters could only be like me. *Blech*. No thank you. There's more than enough of me in this world as it is.

But that's not really what this cliché is about. It's about learning. You can't know about something if you don't first learn. And you can't effectively write about something you know nothing about. It's just logic.

For example, I once encountered a chapter on a writer's forum where the writer wanted feedback on their book. The plot involved a friend stealing the protagonist's book idea and making millions off of it.

Instead of getting into the quality of the content it-self, suffice it to say there's nothing more dull than a writer creating fiction centered on writers. That was one problem, but not a dealbreaker if the writing and plot were strong. Unfortunately, that wasn't the case here.

The actual plot itself was painful proof the writer knew nothing about the publishing process and industry because the scenario laid out was so implausible and preposterous—*implausterous*—it required an audience to suspend all disbelief whatsoever or, frankly, to have a very low IQ.

Forgive me if this comes across a bit harsh, but it needs to be said: You would think that a writer wanting to get published would actually, you know, *learn about the publishing process*, especially when the concept forms the crux of the whole storyline. I'll admit I left very sparse notes because I always try to make sure my writing feedback has some positivity in it—I think I just encouraged the writer to actually research the publishing process.

Therefore, a good writer never stops learning—and the more you learn, the more you have to write about, ergo, the less power writer's block will have over you. Learning is the perfect distraction from writer's block, robbing it of its power and bestowing on you fresh ideas.

These first two clichés line up with what Stephen King teaches in his memoir *On Writing*: "If you want to be a writer, you must do two things above all others:

read a lot and **write a lot**. There's no…shortcut."[1] (Emphasis added.)

Elsewhere in the same book, King says, "Your job isn't to find…ideas but to recognize them when they show up."[2] And it's very hard to do that if you aren't learning. The more you learn, the more you can write. The more you can write, the less you have to worry about writer's block.

CLICHÉ #3: MAKE AN OUTLINE

I've reached a point in my own writing where I pretty much have to make an outline before doing anything else. When I don't make an outline, I usually end up stuck. As soon as I make an outline—*voilá*—unstuck.

An outline is also the best way to maintain focus through a project. Nonfiction writers buy into this pretty easily—chances are, they've already started an outline as part of their research. (I love you so much, nonfiction authors. You're the best.)

Fiction writers…tend to be more stubborn. And I'm including myself here. We often see an outline as stifling to our "creative process." There's a couple of really surprising discoveries I've found by using an outline with fiction, however:

---

[1] Stephen King, *On Writing: A Memoir of the Craft*, (New York: Scribner, 2000), 145

[2] Ibid., 37

<u>SURPRISING DISCOVERY #1</u>
Rather than stifle the creative process, having an outline in fiction writing actually helps you make connections between the beats of your story you might otherwise miss.

<u>SURPRISING DISCOVERY #2</u>
An outline saves the fiction writer from creating incongruities in the plot which would lead to wasted time and effort. The outline serves as not only a guide, but a source of accountability, streamlining the rewriting process.

Outlines aren't very sexy, I know. And I'd be lying to say they are fun. And they're most definitely cliché. But they *are* helpful, and I know I've become a better (and more effective) writer ever since I started implementing them.

I finished the first draft of my first paid screenplay in two and a half weeks, which is lightning fast for those unfamiliar with the film industry. That was while working a full-time sales job and editing a 50,000-plus word book for an independent client. How? You guessed it: I had an outline for the script before writing the first page.

Think of an outline as your literary budget. It shows the balance you start with and what you need to get to the end, and you then think of the various milestones as the "bills" you need to pay along the way. It helps you keep on track so you don't end up in debt at the end of your project. It will help you learn what to trim away—or save for a rainy day.

Any time you're stuck on a new project, you can flip back to your outline as motivation to keep moving forward, thus emasculating any writer's block rearing its ugly head.

If you're not sure where to start with outlining, I'd recommend getting the Storyclock Workbook from Plot Devices.[3] It's a pretty ingenious tool and can be adapted to pretty much any type of writing project imaginable.

There is a hard-to-attribute quote which has a bit of wisdom for us on this very idea: "The secret of getting ahead is getting started. The secret of getting started is breaking your complex overwhelming tasks into small manageable tasks, and then starting on the first one."[4]

Some say this quote belongs to Mark Twain. Others say Agatha Christie or Sally Berger. Whoever said it, it's true. An outline can help you with this very idea—breaking up the complex, overwhelming task of completing the book/novel/opera, etc. into focused chunks that you know you can handle.

Obviously, these aren't the only writing clichés out there, but they are the ones I personally find the most

---

[3] Web address: https://plotdevices.co/products/storyclock-work-book

[4] Quote Investigator, "The Secret of Getting Ahead is Getting Started," QuoteInvestigator.com, February 3, 2018, accessed June 15, 2019, https://quoteinvestigator.com/2018/02/03/start/.

helpful—and they are the easiest to remember. And tips that are easiest to remember are the best ones to draw upon when you find yourself stuck and need a way out.

STRATEGY #2:
the idea bank

"I've often said that there's no such thing as writer's block; the problem is idea block."

-Jeffrey Deaver

There's a good chance this isn't the first time you've heard of an Idea Bank, but that's just proof that it works. One of the many things that is so great about creating an Idea Bank is it's an easy tool that any writer of any level of experience can create. Another one of the great things about it is it carves out an avenue in which the writer can bypass their writer's block.

For those to whom the Idea Bank is a new idea, it's a simple concept with three easy steps:

1. Create a document which exists only as storage for partial stories or half-baked ideas.
2. Paste these ideas into the bank.
3. Just let them sit there while you move on to other, more fully-formed projects.

All writers experience seasons of sudden bursts of creativity which seem to have no end. Well, let me burst the bubble. At some point, the burst will end. And an Idea Bank is a good way to take advantage of the seasons of plenty to prepare for those seasons of famine.

There's a story in the Old Testament of Joseph (and his technicolor dream coat), a young man sold into slavery by his own brothers and then ends up in prison for a crime he didn't commit. I thought I had it bad when my oldest brother forced me to lick his armpit, but Joseph's brotherhood rivalries take the cake.

Don't worry, his story has a happy ending. Joseph is able to get out of prison when he is the only person in the kingdom able to interpret Pharaoh's enigmatic dreams. He predicts Egypt will experience seven plentiful harvests followed by seven years of famine and advises the king to create a system in which they save up during the years of plenty to prepare for the years of famine. Long story, short: Joseph becomes Pharaoh's right-hand man, Egypt becomes a source of food not only for their own people but the surrounding nations, thereby increasing their own influence and wealth. And eventually, Joseph reunites with with his brothers and forgives them for that one time they sold him into slavery.

This story of biblical proportions provides the same basic principles of why every writer should keep an idea bank. During the times of plenty when the ideas are flowing, you don't waste time overthinking a story that's not ready to be written yet. But you also don't completely abandon the idea. You save it for a "rainy" day. The kind of rainy day when writer's block, our ancient foe, rears its ugly head.

I'll get into this more in the next strategy (the Ol' Switcheroo), but you may find the Idea Bank a source of inspiration when you get stuck. You may discover an idea you thought would be its own story would be perfect for the one you are working on and add it into the mix.

In fact, this is how much of my first novel *Dawsun Coppertop* was written. I had gotten stuck on it for a good year and then committed myself to writing it again. But I wasn't sure which way to go. My outline was there (for the most part) but felt thin—I knew I needed more meat on the bones to bring the story to life.

My answers were waiting for me in my Idea Bank. I found in there several story ideas that I had jotted down with the intention of turning into their own stories, but instead, they ended up as full chapters—and new characters—that fit in so well with the novel, it practically felt they were planned that way all along.

Some writers may struggle with knowing when to place an idea in the Idea Bank or when to spend more time developing it right away. At the end of the day, that's something you have to decide for yourself. My best advice is that when you have no clear direction for an idea but want to make sure you don't forget it, then it's the perfect time to make a deposit into your Idea Bank and keep it safe until you need it.

Eventually, the time will come to make a withdrawal, whether you develop it into its own story or incorporate it into an existing one as I did with my first novel. The whole purpose is to give yourself ammunition for future bouts with writer's block. Remember, not all of a farmer's seeds will grow into plants and not all of your ideas will become full-fledged stories. But they could later be re-purposed as a subplot, or several could be combined together to create a new story altogether. In this way, these idea deposits help you move past writer's block and give a project more depth and personality.

ATTENTION! A WORD OF WARNING: Make sure you don't let your Idea Bank become an excuse to not finish a project. You never want a bank that is so full you have no complete works. Otherwise, it's not an Idea Bank—it's a wish list. And while dreams may come true through a combination of hard work, determination, and talent, wishes almost never do. That's right—you can forget about birthday candles, shooting stars, and magical lamps.

Instead of complaining about writer's block, the Idea Bank provides you with an easy and practical tool to spur on your creative juices as needed. And that's a piece of advice you can take to the bank.

Yuck. Forget that last sentence. That was terrible.

STRATEGY #3: the ol' switcheroo

"Two heads are better than none."

-Ethan Coen

The next strategy is going to come across as insane at first. Because, well, it *is* a little insane. It's called "The Ol' Switcheroo," which is my way of saying, don't just work on one project at a time—work on two at a time.

Now, for those struggling with writer's block, I realize how insane this sounds. You might object, "How can I work on two projects when I'm struggling with just one?!" It's a fair question.

But the fact of the matter is that one of the keys for getting out of writer's block—or avoiding it altogether—is to be proactive in your writing approach. You can take steps to prevent it from taking over, but you have to plan ahead. And that's why it never hurts to have more than one iron in the fire.

The Ol' Switcheroo works best when you have two different projects going on at the same time. The idea is to purposefully flip-flop between the two as needed. This may sound counterproductive, but it can actually be really great for spurring on the creative juices.

My opening quote is from Ethan Coen, one-half of the great Coen brothers filmmaking duo. You know them. *Fargo*, *O Brother, Where Art Thou?*, *No Country For Old Men*, *True Grit*. The list goes on. In context, the quote concerns what it's like working with his brother on every project. But I'm using it here to make my own point, because sometimes it's fun to take quotes slightly out of context like that. Also, I believe it has a hidden meaning we can learn from.

It is typical for the Coens to work on one project at a time. However, there are times for exceptions, especially in the creative process, and such was the case when the Coens were writing both *No Country For Old Men*, an adaptation of the excellent crime novel by the same name, and *Burn After Reading*, an original comedy. They alternated between the two screenplays, which is amazing when one considers how very different the two films are from each other in both story and tone.

While my general advice is for writers to be focused on one project at a time so you can give it one hundred percent of your effort and talent and attention, I believe there are times which call for The Ol' Switcheroo. I have had moments when I got stuck on a certain scene or chapter and found the best way to deal with it was to step back and work on something else for a while, especially if the "something else" was completely different.

Rather than stifle my creativity, I find that making this switch helps me rejuvenate, find a new perspective, and return to my original project with gusto and pizzazz. Okay, maybe not pizzazz. But gusto for sure.

The greatest mistake a writer can make when dealing with writer's block is to step away from writing completely. Do you need to take a break sometimes? Sure. But breaks are intended to be short, defined periods of time which allow you rest and rejuvenation—and too often "breaks" turn into an extended leave of absence with no return date.

Even when you're taking a break, you still need to be writing *something*—even if that something will never see the light of day. If nothing else, it can help you get unstuck because it's a low-pressure task. Otherwise, it's too easy to slip into the dark realms of the Undisciplined.

A personal example: when I was writing my first paid screenplay, a true story biopic, I was simultaneously helping a client publish her first book, a collection of fifty memoirs she had collected. Rather than being overwhelming, I found going back-and-forth between these two very different projects helped me stay fresh and keep my mind active. If I got stuck on one, I switched to the other, and vice-versa. Honestly, I don't think I would have finished either project as quickly if I had not used this tactic.

As of the writing of this book, one of those projects has seen the light of day (the book) and the other has not yet (the movie) and probably will not since production stalled out in 2020. But I truly believe the reason I didn't struggle with writer's block on either project was because I was strategically juggling both and doing the Ol' Switcheroo as needed. Also, as I previously mentioned, I had an incredible outline for the film to help me stay motivated.

At the end of the day, your main object is to *finish* your writing, whatever it is. And as counter-intuitive as it may seem, sometimes the best method is the Ol' Switcheroo. My main word of warning with this strategy is not to juggle more than two projects. It you are switching between too many projects, it can turn into a version of procrastinating. You'll feel like you're being productive, but you're really becoming unfocused. I'll raise my own hand as such an offender.

STRATEGY #4:
fake it 'til you make it

"You can always edit a bad page. You can't edit a blank page."

-Jodi Picoult

It took me eleven years to write my first novel *Dawsun Coppertop*. Eleven. That's three different US Presidents in office, mind you. And if you think that sounds impressive, then let me assure you it's not. It's downright shameful. And that's why we need to talk about the importance of perseverance and endurance in the writing process.

Actually, that number is not completely true, depending on how you look at it. It didn't take me eleven years to write the novel. It took me eleven years to write and *release* it. It's one thing for a project to take that long because of doing due diligence and research. It's a whole other story if it takes this long because of fear, as it was in my case. Fear of what? Fear of being read.

I know that sounds insane. Or maybe it doesn't. But when you care so much about something you've written, the idea of it being read and judged by others is a crippling thought. *What if they don't like it? What if I'm not good? What if someone gets offended by the damn cursing?*

Fear can be a root cause for writer's block. Sometimes it is just the manifestation of a latent anxiety within the writer. Fear of rejection. Fear of wasting time. Fear of actually being read, for crying out loud.

I see this fear crop up for a lot of the authors I work with whether they are writing a book themselves or having someone ghostwrite. In their mind, the book is this pure, perfect object. But then when they look at it on the page, they can only see the imperfections, the flaws, and their own uncertainties. I've seen this fear kill projects that otherwise could have really been great.

Author Roy Blount, Jr. offers sage words on this very idea of fear within the writer. "I think writer's block is simply the dread that you are going to write something horrible,"[5] Blount writes. "But as a writer, I believe that if you sit down at the keys long enough, sooner or later something will come out."

Something *will* come out. It might be something good, bad, or ugly, but something will come out. And then you can actually *do* something with it—but we'll get back to that in a minute.

A lot of writers think they have to wait to write until the right moment, some mythical inspirational crescendo

---

[5] The Writer's Circle, "8 Quotes to Combat Writer's Block," Writers-Circle.com, accessed June 15, 2019, https://writerscircle.com/quotes-to-combat-writers-block/.

they will stumble into. They just need to "feel" it. But if you keep waiting to "feel" inspired, inspiration usually transforms into hibernation.

Don't buy into it! There is no magical witching hour of writing. No crucifix to ward off the demons of fear. Sometimes you just have to buckle down and write, write, write. And that's all there is to it. Sheer discipline, willpower, and agonizing perseverance. The hardest part of this is it requires a willingness to look past the flaws you know are there.

Yes, sometimes what you write is going to be really terrible. There's no way around that. No one does good work all the time. There are legends that Shakespeare never crossed out a word he wrote. I believe this for the most part, not because his work is so perfect, but because it's riddled with mistakes. The cost of ink and parchment at that time was so high, you couldn't waste any of it. If you made a mistake, you just kept moving on and dealt with it, and the observant reader of the Bard's works will find examples a-plenty.

For example (did you see that coming?), one of my all-time favorites is in the famous *Romeo and Juliet*. Early on in the play, there is a scene between Juliet, Lady Capulet, and the Nurse. Lady Capulet dismisses the Nurse to leave the room and then almost immediately changes her mind and remembers she needs the Nurse to stay. My two cents is this doesn't read as being an intentional artistic choice, but Shakespeare realizing, "Aw crap, I actually need the Nurse to stay in this scene! Um, what do I do...? A-ha! I still have some room to add to the line here. I'll just have Lady Capulet change her mind. Brilliant!" I know, I know, Elizabethan language sounds so different than our own.

The moral of the story is Shakespeare made his living writing. That's no surprise. Here's another non-surprise: You can't make a living writing if you don't write! You're not going to produce A+ material every time. Shakespeare didn't. So let yourself off the hook, give yourself some grace, and accept the painful but freeing fact you are not perfect. After all, we modern writers have an advantage Shakespeare didn't have: the word processor. Which means we can EDIT to our heart's content.

I love the opening Jodi Picoult quote because, even though I've never read a single book by her (sorry, Jodi), I think it's incisive and wise. A book really comes to life during the editing process, but you can't edit something which hasn't been written.

Do not wait for inspiration to strike. I repeat: do NOT wait for inspiration to strike. Sometimes you just have to write and then revisit the words later through the eyes of an editor instead of an author. I've written scenes before which were incredibly forced, but I had to get something on the page, and then when I came back to the scene a week later, I put on my editor hat and was actually able to transform it into something worth reading.

This is the heart of Fake It 'Til You Make It. Sometimes you just have to fake it when writing. Sometimes you just have to get words on the page even though you know they're not quite right and they lack inspiration.

But it's always better to write three sentences than no

sentences. And even if you end up cutting two of those sentences during the editing process, you still have net gain on your word count!

One of the best ways to achieve this is to set deadlines for yourself. After all, if you were writing for a client, you would have a deadline, so why should your own pursuits be any different? That's the only reason I finally released my novel, to be honest. I set myself a deadline of releasing it on a specific date, no matter what. And I did.

Was it perfect? No. I literally found two typos when I got the first order in. Did I have a launch team or marketing plan ready to go? No. But those are topics for another book to cover.

Not to undersell myself as an editor, but there is no book I've edited that comes out 100% perfect. There are always things I would change. Whether it's because of a formatting issue my client and I both missed during the final read-through or the author makes a choice I personally would not make (because it's their book, not mine), that's just part of the writing and editing process.

Perfection is actually the enemy of accomplishment. I know that sounds backwards, but it is. Every Oscar-winning movie has a mistake in it somewhere, every best-selling book had a typo in its first print, every stage play has an actor who misses a word of a line or forgets a line completely and another actor has to come to the rescue so that the show can go on. Welcome to the Arts. It's not a celebration of what's perfect, it's a celebration of what we create.

I'm not encouraging you to be average in your writing (God forbid), or to "settle" in your writing, but rather to strive for realistic excellence by freeing yourself from the myth of perfection. So Fake It 'Til You Make It, because you will in fact *make* it (whatever your "it" is) with enough focus, determination, and grit.

Notice I didn't mention "talent" in that list. That's because talent can't be taught or acquired. It's inherent. But focus, determination, grit, discipline—those are things that *can* be learned. They are only learned through practice, though—and you know the old cliché: practice makes perfect.

Oops. Did I just contradict myself? I guess this book isn't going to be perfect after all. Oh well, I'll get over it. Maybe I'll just edit out this part later. We'll see.

The bottom line is that editing is where you need to focus. First drafts are first drafts for a reason. They just have to get done before you can do anything else. With enough mental yoga, you can be released from the unrealistic expectation of perfection. Fake It 'Til You Make It and be free to write and then edit until you can't edit anymore.

STRATEGY #5: the magical ingredient

*"Don't try to figure out what other
people want to hear from you; figure
out what you have to say. It's the one
and only thing you have to offer."*
-Barbara Kingsolver

Our last strategy is another cliché, I'm afraid. But it's one so important and powerful that I believe it needed its own section. Despite the eye rolls it may induce, I call it the "Magical Ingredient."

The Magical Ingredient isn't just a strategy for overcoming writer's block, though. I think it is the key to success and to "selling yourself" as a writer. Because people only buy into your words if you have something worth selling.

So here it is. Are you ready? Are you ready for the Magical Ingredient? Alright...

The Magical Ingredient is for you to just be yourself. That's it.

First things first, this is easier said than done. We live in a world saturated with peer pressure. "Buy this. Do this. Be this. Everyone else is!"

It's also very tempting to want to emulate the style and language of writers you admire. I wish I could write like William Faulkner. But I can't, because I'm not William Faulkner, and even if I could write just like him, then everyone would just say, "This guy's a Faulkner ripoff."

We writers put an unfair pressure on ourselves to write as well as our writing idols. And while there's nothing wrong with learning from those idols and emulating parts of their writing if it truly helps you feel inspired, becoming a copycat of someone else rarely produces great results. In fact, it usually leads to greater frustration and more writer's block.

Finding your own voice in your writing is the key to escaping the purgatory of writer's block, though. Much of the time, the reason we get stuck is because we are trying to write like someone else, or hoping we can write like someone else. But comparison is the game of the devil.

Awhile ago, I worked with a client on her first book, which was really daunting for her. For one, it was an autobiography, so she was opening up her life to the whole world. No matter who you are, that's terrifying. For another thing, she wasn't a trained writer and was very open with me about this.

A reading of the first few pages made me realize how much work I had cut out for me. There was a chance I was going to have to even co-author the book to get it to where it needed to be. A few days later, I was wasting time on social media and saw a post from her.

That changed everything. Her writing on the post was fantastic. It sounded like her. It was easy to follow. It had everything her draft was missing in terms of personality and voice. So I wrote her an email. Something along the lines of, "Write every page of your book like a social media post."

I also encouraged her to record herself talking and reading to see how different her first draft was from what was actually on her mind. She just needed a little guidance in being herself and finding her voice.

The year before, I had a similar situation with another author who handed in the first draft of her intro, where the style was incredibly scattered. Some sections were great—I could hear her actually saying those words as if she were in the room. Other sections were far too academic. It felt like I was reading two different authors even though it was just her.

We talked through this problem to get to the root of the issue. She had just started working on her Master's degree and was going back-and-forth between writing her book and writing school papers. So we had to change our strategy because her academic, professional voice from school papers was creeping into her book and it simply didn't belong there. Once she was aware of the problem, she was able to go back and rewrite those sections. The second draft was a vast improvement and actually sounded like her, which was a good thing.

By being yourself in your writing, you give yourself the permission to write the way you want to write, to discover your style and embrace it as unique. So anytime you feel stuck, or you're not sure what to say next, just start writing about how you are stuck and not sure what to say next!

I once had another client who was experiencing writer's block with her chapter endings. She was a great, natural writer and had no problem turning her research and interviews into good material. But she didn't know how to find her voice at the end and communicate her thoughts to her readers.

So my advice to her was to ask herself, "Why did I write this story?" And then answer that question by typing it out. With that simple exercise, she was able to find the words to communicate not just why she had written the story, but why it was important and why her readers should care.

There is a famous Zig Ziglar quote about sales that says, "Selling is essentially a transfer of feelings."[6] I think the same is true of writing. You sell yourself as an author to your reader by transferring over your feelings and thoughts into their head. This is also why Stephen King claims that writing is "telepathy, of course."[7] And I think he's write. I mean, right.

The best advice I received before I went on my first trip to LA to meet with a variety of Hollywood professionals came from a coworker who used to work for one

---

[6] Zig Ziglar, BrainyQuote.com, accessed June 15, 2019, https://www.brainyquote.com/quotes/zig_ziglar_724586.

[7] Stephen King, *On Writing: A Memoir of the Craft*, (New York: Scriber, 2000), 103

of the largest movie studios in the world. "Just be yourself," he said. "And you'll figure out who wants to work with you, and it will give you the discernment to know who you want to work with, too."

Turns out he was right. I went into my first meeting with a potential agent, took a deep breath, and asserted that I would just be myself and answer every question 100 percent honestly, even if I didn't think it was the right answer, that is, the "Hollywood" answer, if you will. What happened? They asked me to be a client on the spot.

Later on, during a pitch to a film producer, I went into the call with the nervous resolve to be myself. I didn't try to impress, I just talked about who I was as a writer and why I wanted to write their film. Two weeks later, I was signing my first movie contract.

Not every pitch meeting has been a success, and I don't want to mislead you that I strike gold every time. I've been told no, too. Sometimes it's just not a fit. That's okay. I wasn't meant to collaborate with those people at that specific time. But I was myself and didn't lose my identity just by trying to impress someone. That charade would have eventually crumbled and burned bridges.

So as cliché and corny as it may sound, that is the Magical Ingredient of overcoming writer's block. Be yourself and write from the heart. That's not always easy, but it *is* possible, and you're the only one who can make it possible.

C.S. Lewis once said, "I wrote the books I should have liked to read if I could have got them. That's always been my reason for writing. People won't write the books

I want, so I have to do it myself."[8] He made himself his audience. And guess what? It worked. He is still one of the most-read authors of the twentieth century, and one of the few to have multiple bestsellers across multiple genres: fantasy (*The Chronicles of Narnia*), science fiction (*Out of the Silent Planet*), theology (*Mere Christianity*), and even autobiographical (*Surprised By Joy*).

So write the kind of books/movies/poems/memoirs that you yourself would buy—and write them as yourself. It is very freeing to be yourself, not just from a mental or emotional standpoint, but from a professional and artistic one as well. I think you'll be pleasantly surprised at how free the words will flow when you find the Magical Ingredient of yourself.

To circle back to the Maya Angelou quote at the start of Strategy #1, what is the story that is burning inside of you? That is the one you should be telling. It doesn't matter if you think it's just silly or selfish or unmarketable. That's the one you should let out to the world.

---

[8] Green and Hooper, *C. S. Lewis: A Biography*, (New York: Harper, 1974), 169.

in conclusion...

I don't really have much to say in conclusion. I'm not saying I have all the answers. I still struggle with writer's block, too—but not nearly as often as I used to thanks to these strategies.

I'm of the opinion that everyone is a storyteller in some shape or fashion. Whether someone is a writer, dancer, pilot, industrial mechanic, vending machine stocker, or salesman, we all write stories every day with every action we take.

Not all stories are good, and I'll never pretend they all are. I won't pretend I like every story either. I have had to force myself through material before—both my own work and others. I've been excited about projects only to later resolve they should not see the light of day. Far from being too self-critical, it's a result of growing in my ability to critique myself and accept criticism.

Speaking of, while this is more-or-less unrelated to writer's block, I think two of the most important traits for anyone is to be humble and be coachable. Don't see a critique—or advice—as a personal attack. See it as an opportunity to grow. Criticism is always better than indifference, in my opinion.

And yes, it has to be constructive criticism. We've all had caustic words from those who would just rather tear down, whether out of jealousy or pure cruelty. That's not what I'm talking about. I'm talking about true criticism from someone who only wants the best for you and wants to help you grow. At the end of the day, those are the people rooting for you to succeed, because they know you are capable of more. If they didn't think so, they would say nothing at all.

We writers can be a difficult bunch. We see our words as our babies and don't always receive criticism well and we can be too quick to defend our work rather than be open-minded enough to say, "Huh, maybe there's something there. Maybe I should reassess that."

When you can become more receptive to criticism, quicker to listen than to retort, your writing can't help but improve.

If, on the other hand, you can't take advice and feedback from others, you will run the extreme risk of writing lots of words no one will ever want to read. In my opinion, that's actually worse than writer's block.

You might overcome all the trials and travails of writer's block, escape from PurgaStory and create an incredible masterpiece that none of your friends buy. Don't let that surprise or dishearten you. You will actually be better off if your audience is rooted outside of your friend group. In the long run, it will work out for the better.

Above all else, I hope this guide has been helpful and not a waste of your (or my) time. I would love to hear what strategies you used to overcome writer's block, or if none of my strategies worked, you're always welcome to curse me under your breath. You can find me on Instagram as @jonathan.jordan.writer or better yet, sign up for my newsletter where I share additional thoughts on writing.

For now, it's time to bring this to a close and move on to the next idea. There is no end to the words we can use to express our thoughts, feelings, and hopes, and that is what makes writing so beautiful.

Need Some Writing Encouragement?
Subscribe here to receive some.

wordrobemedia.com/newsletter

bibliography

Green, Lancelyn and Walter Hooper. *C.S. Lewis: A Biography.* New York: Harper, 1974.

King, Stephen. *On Writing: A Memoir of the Craft.* New York: Scribner, 2000.

Quote Investigator. "The Secret of Getting Ahead is Getting Started." QuoteInvestigator.com. February 3, 2018. Accessed June 15, 2019. https://quoteinvestigator.com/2018/02/03/start/.

Writer's Circle, The. "8 Quotes To Combat Writers Block." WritersCircle.com. Accessed June 15, 2019. https://writerscircle.com/quotes-to-combat-writers-block/.

Zig Ziglar Quotes. BrainyQuote.com, BrainyMedia Inc, 2019, accessed June 15, 2019, https://www.brainyquote.com/quotes/zig_ziglar_724586.

ABOUT THE AUTHOR

Jonathan Jordan (born circa 1985 AD) believes in the power of stories and words as they depict and define humanity's best and worst and have the pseudo-magical ability to inspire the human imagination.

He earned a degree in English Literature, spent eight years as a social worker, and founded Wordrobe Media, dedicated to telling stories through book coaching, screenwriting, and media production. He lives near Dallas in the great nation of Texas with his beautiful wife (who is also a writer) and their two sons.

He is also the co-host of two podcasts:
The Games Odyssey (History of the Olympic & Paralympic Games)
Magical Movie Marathon (Watching through the entire Disney Animated Canon)

Check out more at Wordrobe Media.

www.ingramcontent.com/pod-product-compliance
Lightning Source LLC
Chambersburg PA
CBHW051401250726
48656CB00006B/2217